Grand Canyon
impressions

photography by Bernadette Heath

FARCOUNTRY
PRESS

"To my backpacking, river-rafting, horseback-riding friends, may we soar again."
Thank you to JANET WEBB FARNSWORTH, who wrote the captions.

Right: Howlands Butte bears the name of two brothers, Oramel and Seneca, members of Major John Wesley Powell's famous 1869 exploration of the Colorado River. Growing discouraged, the Howland brothers, along with another expedition member, William Dunn, left the group at a site now called Separation Canyon. The three men are believed to have been killed by Indians shortly after.

Title page: White storm clouds hover above the Inner Gorge, the deepest portion of the Grand Canyon. Here, the Colorado River cuts its way through the Vishnu Schist, the oldest and deepest rock unit in the Canyon.

Front cover: Sun glimmering on golden buttes, a brief snowstorm pelting a side canyon, and the ever-changing interplay of sunlight and shadows all contribute to the mystique of the Grand Canyon.

Back cover: Blooming flowers, quiet pools, and tumbling waterfalls show the softer side of the Grand Canyon.

ISBN: 1-56037-367-9
Photography © 2005 by Bernadette Heath
© 2005 Farcountry Press

For more information about our books write Farcountry Press, P.O. Box 5630, Helena, MT 59604; call (800) 821-3874; or visit www.farcountrypress.com.

Created, produced, and designed in the United States. Printed in China.

In the winter of 1858, the exploratory excursion of Joseph Christmas Ives, 1st Lieutenant of the U.S. Army's Corps of Topographical Engineers, snaked up the Colorado River to the western edge of Grand Canyon. Unable to navigate further, he and his men continued over land and descended a harrowing route to the Canyon floor. Frustrated by frequent obstacles and an apparent lack of exploitable natural resources, Ives observed, "The region…is, of course, altogether valueless. Ours has been the first, and will doubtless be the last, party of whites to visit this profitless locality." He has since been proven wrong, in spectacular fashion, on both counts.

In fact, they were not the first "whites" to arrive. Spanish explorers preceded Ives and his party by more than three centuries. Nor were they the last. Grand Canyon National Park is one of the most heavily visited national parks in the country, playing host to over four million visitors annually. It is considered one of the Seven Natural Wonders of the World and one of the "crown jewels" of the National Park System.

Equally erroneous was Ives' description of the canyon as a "profitless locality." The revenue generated by future tourism alone would have been unimaginable to a man of his time. Vacationing in exotic places was an activity available to only the wealthy in the nineteenth century. In the span of a few generations, however, tourism became affordable to the larger population. Today, visitors to Grand Canyon National Park pump millions of dollars into the regional economy each year. To be fair, when speaking of a profit motive, Ives was likely referring to the absence of raw materials such as extractable minerals or timber. But even on this note he was incorrect. Miners have extracted a variety of minerals from Grand Canyon including high-grade copper ore, uranium, asbestos, and silver, and the North Rim (far above Ives' vantage) is home to a dense, old-growth forest.

In the final analysis, the Grand Canyon's "worth" is truly incalculable. There are few destinations around the globe with more compelling natural and cultural resources, or greater opportunity to experience unspoiled wilderness, than the world's most famous chasm. For these reasons, the United Nations has declared Grand Canyon a World Heritage Site. This designation proclaims the Grand Canyon to be of outstanding importance to the common heritage of humankind. The Grand Canyon and the Colorado River, which both carves and nourishes, provide critical habitat for myriad species of flora and fauna—from an indigenous and endangered fish called the humpback chub to the equally rare California condor. Geologists have long flocked to the canyon to study one of North America's most intact, visible geologic records—uncovering the ancient secrets, exposed by six million years of erosion, of our continent and planet. In terms of cultural significance, there are at least seven American Indian tribes that have existing or ancestral ties to the Grand Canyon.

Among them are the Hopi, whose ancestors inhabited the canyon's fertile deltas and precipitous cliffs for centuries before making a mysterious exodus in the 1200s, and the Havasupai, who still dwell amidst the tumbling blue-green waterfalls of Havasu Creek in western Grand Canyon.

Many forward-thinking luminaries have understood the significance of this multi-layered marvel and have dedicated their lives to preserving the experience for others to enjoy. Most notably was President Theodore Roosevelt, who declared the Grand Canyon a national monument in 1908. His famous quote is oft-repeated by canyon lovers of all stripes: "In the Grand Canyon, Arizona has a natural wonder which so far as I know, is in kind absolutely unparalleled throughout the rest of the world…. Leave it as it is. You cannot improve on it. The ages have been at work on it, and man can only mar it. What you can do is to keep it for your children, your children's children, and for all who come after you."

The National Park Service, which has administered the Grand Canyon since President Woodrow Wilson declared it a national park in 1919, has recently identified a number of "parkwide interpretive themes." These broad categories try to distill that which makes Grand Canyon so special, and so worthy of federal protection. My personal favorite, summarized in a word, is "inspiration." For thousands of years, visionaries and visitors alike have been inspired by the unique phenomenon that Major John Wesley Powell, arguably the first to travel through the canyon by river in 1869, named the Grand Canyon.

How are visitors inspired by Powell's canyon? Some might be seated on the rim, watching cloud shadows sweep across any of the hundreds of peaks and "temples" that populate the inner canyon, or find themselves hiking from top to bottom, trading boreal forest for desert scrub in fewer than a dozen miles. Others might be running the challenging whitewater of the Colorado River, aware that this thin but mighty river is the lifeblood of the American Southwest. Still others may be in the saddle en route to legendary Phantom Ranch, or high above in a sightseeing helicopter, or even continents away,

turning the pages of a picture book, presented with a kaleidoscope of the sublime and majestic.

Whatever one's method of connection, the canyon has an unfailing ability to transform whoever opens themselves to its messages. A nearly universal reaction is to find one's idea of self shrinking into insignificance when confronted by the immense scale of the commanding gorge. Another is the sense of accomplishment after successfully negotiating the canyon's forbidding terrain. In my ten years as a year-round resident, I've seen visitors gape, cry, laugh, swoon, and cartoonishly rub their eyes in disbelief. Rare is the onlooker that is not moved in some way, whether it is their first or fiftieth encounter. Though sight is not the only sense that one brings to bear when contemplating the canyon, it is arguably the most likely to overwhelm.

The canyon has many signature smells, sounds, textures and tastes. But there is little substitute for the impact that a visual study can provide.

In this collection of images, Bernadette Heath has found a way to share her unique impressions of Grand Canyon. Her vision manifests itself in the small and the large, the intimate and profound. As a fellow photographer and backcountry enthusiast, I have admired her photography for years. Bernadette's forays from rim to river have resulted in an impressive body of work that demonstrates an enlightened eye when it comes to capturing many of the canyon's moods and melodies.

MIKE BUCHHEIT
Grand Canyon National Park resident, Director of Grand Canyon Field Institute, and freelance writer/photographer

Above: This red-orange Indian paintbrush is nestled amidst a clump of sage.

Facing page: Hermit Creek, with its small cascading waterfalls, is named for Louis D. Boucher, known as "the hermit." He operated a copper mine and a tourist camp in the area in the late nineteenth century.

Above: Havasu Creek forms one of the Park's most scenic side canyons and is home to the Havasupai Indians. In the Havasupai language, havasu means "blue-green water," a reference to the color of the mineral-rich water that has carved this unique side canyon.

Left: Columbus Point is bathed in morning sunlight, while Hermit Creek Trail is still in shade. This historic trail drops 4,240 feet from the South Rim.

Above: These quaint cabins accommodate visitors to the North Rim. More luxurious accommodations can be found at nearby Grand Canyon Lodge. The North Rim has the peaceful advantage of fewer visitors than the more accessible South Rim.

Left: Monkey flowers tenaciously grow in the Grand Canyon's rocky soil. A member of the figwort family, the plant blooms in the spring; this one adds a dash of color to a white cliff.

Facing page: Mirror-like Grapevine Creek reflects the tall cliffs that surround it. It is not known how the creek got its name, but it is thought that the moniker came from the wild grapes growing in the drainage.

Above: Prehistoric pictographs are hidden inside a small cave in Chamberlain Canyon. Difficult to accurately date, these images are estimated to be more than one thousand years old. Their exact meaning is unknown, but some experts speculate they were part of religious or hunting ceremonies.

Left: A dirt road leads through the Kaibab National Forest to Point Sublime on the North Rim. In 1880, geologist and author Clarence E. Dutton described the view from the canyon overlook as "the most sublime and awe-inspiring spectacle in the world."

Above: The flat surface of the Tonto Platform is a favorite resting place for hikers along the Tonto Trail. The landform is named for the Tonto-Apache Indians.

Facing page: This majestic view of Bright Angel Canyon, as seen from near Bright Angel Point on the North Rim, showcases the Canyon's splendor. A multitude of side canyons make their way to the Colorado River to form this unrivaled wonder.

Above: Hopi House was designed by architect Mary Colter for the Fred Harvey Company. Constructed in 1905 to resemble authentic Hopi buildings at Old Oraibi, the structure now houses a Native American arts and crafts market.

Left: Grandview Trail was constructed in 1892 by miners. A few deserted mines remain where the trail reaches Horseshoe Mesa.

Above: A tiny five-needle fetid marigold finds a hold amid the white stones and red sand.

Left: At 8,255-feet, Bright Angel Point is a favorite viewing spot for visitors to the North Rim.

Above left: The bluish-purple spikes of lupine signal summer on the South Rim.

Above right: The heavy flowers of the Whipple yucca grace one of the most useful cacti growing in the region. Its leaves were used by early Native American tribes to make sandals, ropes, mats, baskets, and other household items.

Right: Winter brings a different spirit to the Grand Canyon. Seen here from the South Kaibab Trailhead on the South Rim, it is hard to imagine that the temperature on the Canyon floor is comparable to that of Phoenix.

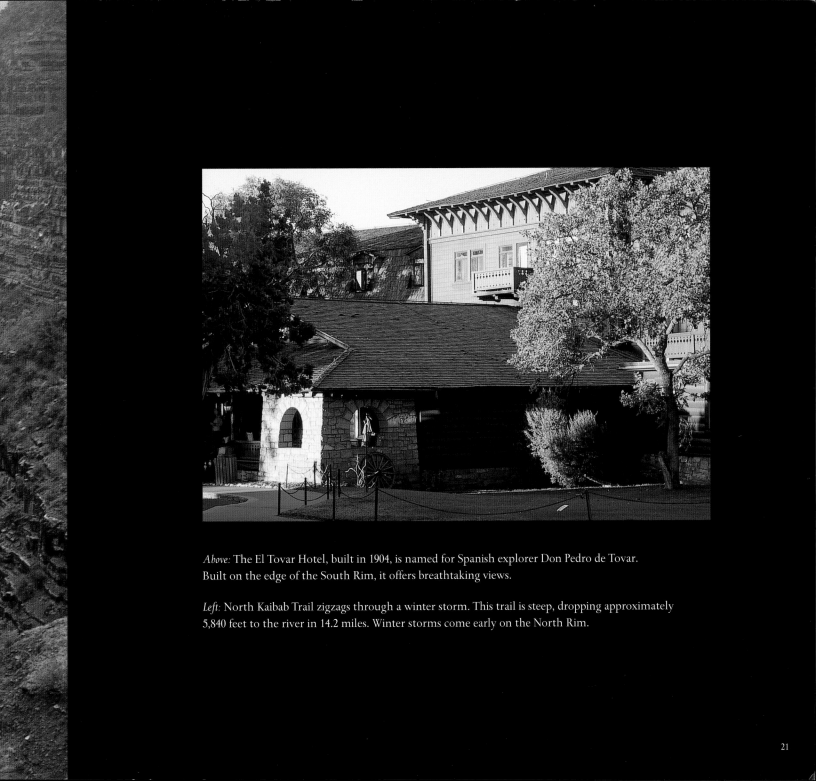

Above: The El Tovar Hotel, built in 1904, is named for Spanish explorer Don Pedro de Tovar. Built on the edge of the South Rim, it offers breathtaking views.

Left: North Kaibab Trail zigzags through a winter storm. This trail is steep, dropping approximately 5,840 feet to the river in 14.2 miles. Winter storms come early on the North Rim.

Left: Zoroaster Temple is dappled in sun and shade as clouds cross the Canyon. This prominent butte, seen from Yaki Point on the South Rim, was named in 1902 for a Persian religious leader.

Below: Mule deer are plentiful on both the North and South Rims.

Above: Colorado means "red" in Spanish. Early travelers quipped that the waters of the Colorado River were "too thick to drink and too thin to plow."

Facing page: Early miners built many of the trails into the Grand Canyon. Here, on Horseshoe Mesa, sandstone walls and an ore bucket are all that remain of a miner's mess hall. The prospectors found lead, zinc, copper, and asbestos in the Canyon.

Above: Lookout Studio is another building designed by architect Mary Colter. Constructed of native stones to blend with the Canyon, it is now a gift shop in addition to being a favorite viewpoint.

Facing page: Hikers participating in an orienteering class study their maps while sitting on 7,260-foot Yaki Point. This class and others are offered by the Grand Canyon Field Institute and help visitors gain a better understanding of the Grand Canyon.

Facing page: Phantom Ranch, designed by architect Mary Colter, was built in 1922. Because of its remote location near the bottom of the Grand Canyon, the ranch receives its supplies by mule.

Below: Bright Angel Creek was named by explorer Major John Wesley Powell.

Above: Redwall Cavern is a favorite stopping spot for rafters on the Colorado River. This limestone amphitheater is yet another feature named by Major John Wesley Powell, who described it as a "vast half-circular chamber." Powell estimated that it could hold fifty-thousand people. Not nearly that large, it does dwarf rafters standing at the opening. The only way to reach Redwall Cavern is by boat.

Facing page: Running from the South Rim to the Colorado River, Monument Creek nourishes the moss that clings to the Canyon walls.

Above: The North Kaibab Trail drops off the North Rim. After crossing over the Colorado River on a suspension bridge, hikers can then climb up the South Kaibab Trail, making a "rim-to-rim" hike.

Right: Pima Point, at 6,798 feet, as seen from Monument Creek.

Right: Cedar Ridge, approximately two miles below the South Rim, receives its name from the many cedars (actually Utah junipers) that cluster near the edge.

Below: Deer Creek Falls plunges nearly one hundred feet to a calm pool below.

Above: Over millions of years, wind and water have worn this stone smooth and carved a small overhang. During a rainstorm, a waterfall cascades over the rock, continuing the process of erosion. Known as Pipe Spring, this spot is located along the Tonto Trail.

Right: Aspen trees display their fall finery near Point Imperial. At 8,803 feet, Point Imperial is the highest spot in the Park.

Left: Considered one of the most exciting whitewater stretches in the Canyon, Hermit Rapids offers a thrilling ride.

Below: Stately Wotans Throne overlooks the wide chasm.

Facing page: A visitor standing at the East Rim is dwarfed by the immensity of the Grand Canyon.

Below: This stone fireplace is the focal point of Hermit's Rest, another of architect Mary Colter's creations.

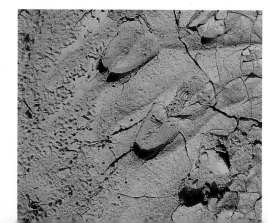

Above: Newberry Butte is named for John S. Newberry, naturalist and physician for the Ives Expedition (1858-59).

Left: Bighorn sheep have left their mark in the red mud of a side canyon.

Facing page: Designed by Mary Colter in 1932 to resemble the ancestral Puebloan (Anasazi) structures in the Four Corners region, the Watchtower seems to stand guard over the Canyon on the east end.

Above: Rafters stop for a lunch break in Marble Canyon. Rafting the
Colorado River is a wild, wet, and wondrous ride through the chasm.

Facing page: From the Tonto Platform, hikers can enjoy a dramatic
view of 83-mile Rapid on the Colorado River.

Facing page: Sunrise at Yavapai Point is an awe-inspiring sight. The rising sun highlights the buttes and formations of this wonderland.

Right: Designed by Mary Colter for the Fred Harvey Company, Bright Angel Lodge was built in 1935. The immense fireplace is the centerpiece of the lobby.

Below: One of many surprises in Surprise Canyon—a tiny canyon tree frog blends in with the surrounding river stones.

Above: The dagger-like leaves of a Utah agave plant (also known as the century plant) are silhouetted against the setting sun. After approximately twelve to fifteen years, the century plant sends up a flowering stalk about fifteen feet high. The plant blooms once then dies.

Right: Hermit Creek plunges over the cliffs to the rocks below. Flooding through this creek pushes boulders into the Colorado River, forming Hermit Rapids.

Right: Angel's Window is a favorite photographic point on the North Rim. Eroded by wind and water, the opening cuts through the Kaibab limestone, the uppermost layer of the Grand Canyon rock formations. In the distance are the San Francisco Peaks.

Below: Sandstone walls are all that remain of an ancestral Puebloan (Anasazi) site in Marble Canyon.

Left: A shy bighorn sheep peeks from behind a tree. These agile animals are at home in the Canyon's steep terrain.

Facing page: Ponderosa pines and Indian paintbrush grow on the lip of Little Dragon Mesa on the North Rim. The flat top of the South Rim looms across the canyon.

Below: Sunrise slowly creeps into Galloway Canyon, named for an early trapper. In the foreground, sage and prickly pear cacti cling to the rocky slopes.

Left: Double rainbows grace Point Sublime. Summer monsoons bring rain during July and August, producing magnificent thunderstorms over the Canyon.

Below: Indian paintbrush line Hermit Trail near Columbus Point.

Above: The "end of the line" for the Grand Canyon Railway is this historic depot of log construction in Grand Canyon Village.

Left: Mather Point provides the perfect spot to view O'Neill Butte, named for William "Bucky" O'Neill, who was killed at the Battle of San Juan Hill in the Spanish-American War.

Above: The Grand Canyon Lodge sits regally at 8,255 feet on the North Rim. Due to heavy snowfall, the North Rim and all visitor services are closed during the winter months.

Facing page: The 6,076-foot Tower of Ra juts skyward. This unique pinnacle is named for the Egyptian sun god.

Above: Gum from the brittlebush was once chewed or used as incense by local tribes.

Left: Looking south from Lonetree Creek on the Tonto Platform, the buttes are given extra drama by the day's first light. Catclaws bloom in the foreground.

Right: Here, the Grand Canyon widens and opens to scenic Lake Mead, which offers almost unlimited opportunities for outdoor recreation.

Below: This narrow slot canyon in Monument Creek provides pools for bathing and warm rocks for drying—a treat for backpackers at Monument Creek campsite.

Facing page: An overlook near Grapevine Creek shows the sheer barrenness of the Granite Gorge. In 1869, explorer Major John Wesley Powell wrote: "We can see but a little way into the granite gorge, but it looks threatening."

Below: Flash floods in Monument Creek have formed natural dams. Known as "the loft," the small dam becomes a waterfall during wet weather.

Right: The massive wall of The Abyss is where Monument Creek begins.

Below: Burro Springs furnishes enough water to produce green vegetation on an otherwise brown hillside. There are two theories about what, or who, it was named after: the area's many wild burros; or a Havasupai guide known as Captain Burro.

Facing page: Serene Vista Encantada in fall is an impressive sight.

Right: Surprise Canyon is an oasis of simple grace. Farther up the creek is Surprise Valley, named by a Powell Expedition photographer who happened upon a spectacular hanging garden.

Above: Grand Canyon Railway locomotives first reached the South Rim in 1901, opening a new chapter in Grand Canyon visitation.

Right: A young mule deer grazes at the Grand Canyon Village on the South Rim.

Facing page: A small trickle of water flows over Matkatamiba Falls, only to disappear in the thirsty sand. This very narrow canyon was named after a Havasupai family. Rafters have nicknamed it Matkat. STEVE MILLER PHOTO

Above: On the South Rim east of Grandview Point, visitors can see Sinking Ship, named for its distinctive shape.

Left: Mount Hayden, as seen from Point Imperial.

Above: The Battleship is located between Indian Gardens and Horn Creek on the Tonto Platform.

Facing page: Point Sublime is an ideal spot to experience the inner canyon.

Above: A Colorado 4 o'clock daintily spreads across the rocks in Marble Canyon.

Right: Navajo Point on the South Rim looks down to Tanner Canyon. Easily reached by Desert View Drive, Navajo Point sits at 7,461 feet.

Above: A California condor displays its unique profile against a Kaibab limestone formation on the South Rim. The endangered species has been reintroduced into northern Arizona and often can be seen soaring on the thermal currents above the Canyon.

Left: A snowstorm enshrouds the South Rim near Boucher Creek, named for Louis D. Boucher. Originally from Quebec, Boucher built a trail from the South Rim to bring supplies to, and take ore out of, his copper mine.

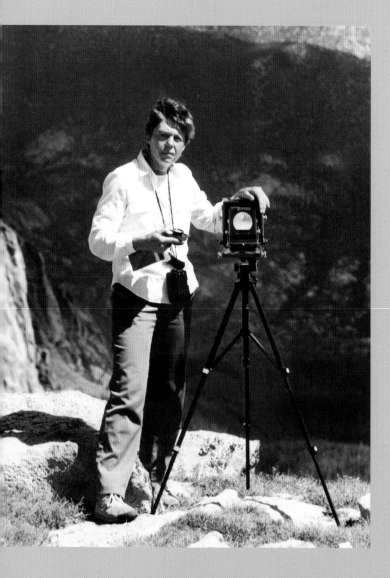

BERNADETTE HEATH. Multimedia artist Bernadette Heath brings to photography her experience in many other aspects of the art world. Using nature as her model, she first created with pen and ink, watercolor, clay, and glass. When she moved to the Southwest, it seemed natural for her to pick up a camera and hike off into the mountains. Working with light, forms, shadows, color, people, animals, and passion are all the elements in fine art.

Heath's photographs have been published in *Arizona Highways Magazine, National Geographic, National Geographic Adventure, Cerca Magazine, Audubon, National Wildlife Federation, American Forests, AAA Highroads,* and *Elle Decor Magazine.* Her work has also appeared in books published by the Western National Park Association, Arizona Highways, Rio Nuevo Publishers, Farcountry Press, Newbridge Publishing, McRae Books Srl, Madden Publishing, and Starlight Publishing. Heath has received awards from the National Federation of Press Women and the SATW Bill Muster Photo Showcase. AgPix.com. www.BernadetteHeath.com